WILL YOU INTERCEDE?

As long as there is an intercessor, there is hope

D1714418

WILL YOU INTERCEDE?

AS LONG AS THERE IS AN INTERCESSOR, THERE IS HOPE

DEREK PRINCE

WILL YOU INTERCEDE?

© 2013 Derek Prince Ministries–International

This edition published by DPM-UK 2021

All rights reserved.

ISBN 978-1-78263-747-9
ePub 978-1-78263-748-6
Kindle 978-1-78263-749-3
Product code T21

This book was compiled from the extensive archive of Derek Prince's unpublished materials and edited by the Derek Prince Ministries editorial team.

www.derekprince.com

CONTENTS

Foreword

Derek Prince believed in intercession—teaching on the topic, writing about it in books and articles, and involving himself personally in it as an expression of his service to the Lord. He also lined up with others who believed that intercession was a practice the Lord could use to change history. And so it has.

From November 21–24 in 1973, Derek Prince was one of the main speakers at a national leadership conference at the Deauville Hotel in Miami Beach, Florida. The event was sponsored by Christian Growth Ministries, publishers of *New Wine* magazine, an international Christian publication.

Joining Derek on the speakers' platform for that conference were Don Basham, David

Edwards and Ern Baxter—and the teaching that came forth during that gathering was rich and substantive. But it was a special meeting of a handful of dedicated Christians during the days of that conference which would bring about the birth of a significant new organization encouraging intercessory prayer.

Earlier in 1973, Derek had released his landmark book, *Shaping History through Prayer and Fasting.* So his attendance at the small gathering of intercessors made sense. All the delegates coalesced around the concept that if nations were to be changed, it would happen only through persistent prayer and intercession. Out of that common agreement was birthed an organization which marked its beginning in late November 1973: Intercessors for America.

Derek Prince was one of that organization's original founders, along with John Talcott (who would become the founding president of IFA), John Beckett, Jay Fesperman, John Heard, George Gillies and Warren Black—all representatives of the business community as well as the religious community. The organization was destined to expand internationally from those small beginnings—spreading its influence to other nations and continuing strong from that day to the present.

Scripture admonishes us in Zechariah 4:10 (NLT): "Do not despise these small beginnings [the day of small things, NIV], for the LORD rejoices to see the work begin." Surely the Lord was rejoicing that day in late November 1973, as this group was formed to spread the principles of intercessory prayer.

It is impossible to know exactly what changes in history, both great and small, have resulted from the intercessory prayers of believers in every nation of the world. In honor of that labor of love, we are pleased to present this book containing a portion of Derek Prince's teaching on this vital topic of intercession. It is our hope that what you read will encourage, affirm and inspire you.

We dedicate this book to you—and to every person in every part of the world who has answered God's call to pray and intercede. Only in heaven will we fully comprehend all that has been accomplished by your dedicated, selfless service in prayer.

This book is for you.

THE INTERNATIONAL PUBLISHING TEAM
OF DEREK PRINCE MINISTRIES

INTRODUCTION

In this book, I want to focus on one of the highest and most powerful ministries open to any Christian: the ministry of intercession. I believe this ministry is God's answer to problems that cannot be resolved in any other way, problems in the lives of individuals or in families or the problems of whole nations.

First of all, let's define what is meant by intercession. The word *intercession* in English actually comes from a Latin root which means "to come in between." In the other languages that are relevant to Scripture—both Hebrew and Greek—the word has basically the same meaning: "to come in between." An intercessor is one who comes in between.

"In between" whom or what? The answer is

that the intercessor comes in between God and the objects of God's just wrath and judgment. The intercessor stands before God, taking a position between the Lord and those who deserve His wrath and judgment. By so doing, the intercessor says, in effect, "God, I acknowledge Your justice. You have every right to smite these people. But if You smite them, You are going to have to smite me too, because I'm standing in between You and them."

That is the role of the intercessor. And that will be the focus of this book.

CHAPTER ONE

The Example of Abraham

To begin our study of this theme of intercession, we will look at a number of the Lord's servants who played the role of intercessors. You will find that all of them were people close to the heart of God. In fact, I believe this particular posture—this ministry of intercession—is something very, very close to the heart of God.

The first example we will look at is that of Abraham interceding on behalf of the city of Sodom. Sodom was a very wicked city and ripe for God's judgment. In the eighteenth chapter of Genesis, we read how the Lord had come to visit Abraham. The Lord had two angels with Him, and Abraham welcomed them and entertained them.

In due course, they gave Abraham the promise of the heir that was to come: Isaac.

As they were getting ready to move on, the Lord told Abraham, "I'm going on to have a look at the city of Sodom for Myself to see if it's really as bad as the reports I've heard about it." At this point, we will look at Genesis 18, beginning at verse 17:

> The Lord said, "Shall I hide from Abraham what I am about to do . . .?* [A Scripture passage in Amos 3:7 says that God will do nothing except He reveals His secrets to His prophets. Abraham was a prophet, so God wanted to share His counsel, His purposes and His thoughts with him.] *And the Lord said, "The outcry of Sodom and Gomorrah is indeed great, and their sin is exceedingly grave. I will go down now, and see if they have done entirely according to its outcry, which has come to Me; and if not, I will know." Then the men turned away from there and went toward Sodom, while Abraham was*

still standing before the LORD. [Please notice those words: "Abraham was standing before the LORD." He was standing between the Lord and the city of Sodom, which was the object of God's pending judgment.] *Abraham came near and said, "Will You indeed sweep away the righteous with the wicked? Suppose there are fifty righteous within the city; will You indeed sweep it away and not spare the place for the sake of the fifty righteous who are in it? Far be it from You to do such a thing, to slay the righteous with the wicked, so that the righteous and the wicked are treated alike. Far be it from You! Shall not the Judge of all the earth deal justly?"*

Notable Points

Having read this passage, I now want to point out the main features of this situation and their implications for intercession. I have already suggested that we need to see Abraham's posture. He was standing before the Lord—standing between the Lord and Sodom, as it were. He was, in effect, holding up his hand and saying, "Lord, don't go any farther."

Next, we want to notice Abraham's intimacy with the Lord. Elsewhere in Scripture, Abraham is called the friend of the Lord (Isaiah 40:8). Here in Genesis 18, Abraham was talking to Almighty God as an intimate and personal friend.

We also need to notice Abraham's boldness. He was actually challenging God's righteousness. He was not afraid to speak out and say what he thought—yet at the same time with holy reverence.

Then, we need to notice as well that Abraham had an absolute conviction of God's justice, both positive and negative. Negatively, that God would punish the wicked; positively, that God would not deal with the righteous as with the wicked. That element is an essential part of the ministry of an intercessor: a conviction of God's absolute justice.

The Conversation Continues

Having established these points, let's now read how the conversation proceeded in Genesis 18:26–33:

So the LORD said, "If I find in Sodom fifty righteous within the city, then I will spare the whole place on their account." And Abraham replied, "Now behold, I have ventured to speak to the Lord, although I am but dust and ashes. Suppose the fifty righteous are lacking five, will You destroy the whole city because of five?" And He said, "I will not destroy it if I find forty-five there." He [Abraham] spoke to Him yet again and said, "Suppose forty are found there?" And [the Lord] said, "I will not do it on account of the forty." Then [Abraham] said, "Oh may the Lord not be angry, and I shall speak; suppose thirty are found there?" And [the Lord] said, "I will not do it if I find thirty there." And [Abraham] said, "Now behold, I have ventured to speak to the Lord; suppose twenty are found there?" And [the Lord] said, "I will not destroy it on account of the twenty." Then [Abraham] said, "Oh may the Lord not be angry, and I shall speak only this once; suppose ten are found there?" And [the Lord] said, "I will not destroy it on ac-

count of the ten." As soon as He had finished
speaking to Abraham the LORD *departed;*
and Abraham returned to his place.

From this passage, I want to highlight two
additional points. The first is that God responds
to the prayer of His servant. God did not brush
Abraham aside. He listened. In a certain sense,
He allowed His course of action to be influenced
by what Abraham said to Him. Think of both the
privilege and the responsibility of being able to
speak to God in such a way that we actually influence His course of action!

Second, we note that God delights to show
mercy. The Lord came down, step by step, from
promising to show mercy if there were fifty to
the last promise He made. The Lord said He
would show mercy if there were only ten righteous persons in that entire wicked city. At the
end of the conversation, the Lord promised He
would spare the entire city of Sodom if He found
ten righteous persons in it.

This story raised a question in my mind
some years ago about the probable population of

Sodom in the days of Abraham. After some considerable research, I came to the conclusion that, at a minimum, there must have been at least ten thousand persons in Sodom at that time. So, ten persons could cause God to spare a city of at least ten thousand. That gives us an interesting proportion: one to a thousand. One righteous person can ward off God's judgment from a thousand wicked persons.

Salt of the Earth

This proportion we are discussing brings me back to the illustration of salt that I have highlighted in other books and messages. Jesus said we are the salt of the earth (Matthew 5:13). There are at least two functions of salt: first of all, to give flavor to that which would otherwise lack flavor; and second, to hold back the process of corruption. As we know, salt is not dumped out in one lump or one big portion in one place. Rather it is scattered in little grains across whatever has to be salted. That is how we Christians are. Each of us may be just a little grain of salt. But we should be holding back the process of corruption, recommending the particular area of the earth where we live to God's mercy and to God's favor.

Let me pose a question here. Is your life so upright before God that your very presence would hold back God's judgment from the entire community or area where you live?

The Impact We Make

We need to take into account the tremendous influence that righteous persons can have in the world today. Their impact is felt in two ways: by their prayers, and by their presence. By our prayers we, like Abraham, can stand between God and the objects of His just wrath and hold off His judgment. By our very presence we commend the area where we are—the community, the society—to God's mercy and God's favor.

Our presence can cause God to hold back His righteous judgment from an entire community or city or even an entire nation. Alternatively, if we are passive and indifferent we will make no impact. In fact, such a lack of response in the face of evil is sinful. James 4:17 says:

Therefore, to one who knows the right thing to do and does not do it, to him it is sin.

That Scripture really faces us with a clear choice. Are we going to commit ourselves to be righteous persons, prayer warriors, intercessors, holding off God's wrath and judgment on our nation? Or are we going to be passive and indifferent, failing to do what the situation demands?

CHAPTER TWO
Moses, the Intercessor

In chapter one, we dealt with the example of Abraham interceding on behalf of Sodom. We saw our "father in the faith" in the posture that typifies the intercessor—the one who stands in between. Abraham was standing before the Lord, standing between God and the object of God's just wrath, which at that moment was the city of Sodom.

In particular, I singled out three features of Abraham's character and relationship with God. First, his intimacy with God; second, his boldness; and third, his conviction of God's absolute justice—both positive and negative. The positive—that God would spare the righteous; the negative—that God would judge the wicked.

I also pointed out two aspects of God's character revealed by this incident. First, that God responds to the prayers of His servant; and second, that God delights to show mercy if we pray.

Mountain Top, Mountain Bottom

In this chapter, our lesson on the power of intercession will be taken from the life of Moses. We begin with an incident where Moses had been up at the top of Mount Sinai—communing with God. Moses had received from God the revelation of His purpose and plan for the future of Israel.

At a certain point in this communion between God and Moses, the Lord changed the direction of the conversation. He told Moses that while they had been together at the top of the mountain, the Israelites down at the foot of the mountain had turned aside from the Lord. They had deviated from the way God had set before them and had gone into idolatry. In fact, they had actually made a golden calf and were worshiping it at that very moment while Moses was up there with the Lord at the top of the mountain.

The Lord's attitude was, "Moses, leave Me alone. I'll destroy this people and I'll make a greater nation out of you." We will now read the words that describe the incident, beginning in Exodus 32:7:

> *Then the LORD spoke to Moses, "Go down at once, for your people, whom you brought up from the land of Egypt, have corrupted themselves."*

Let me point out something that is almost comical in the midst of this intensely serious situation. Neither the Lord nor Moses would accept responsibility at this point for Israel. Each of them was thoroughly disgusted with Israel.

The Lord said to Moses, "Your people, whom you brought up." A little later in the passage, we see Moses saying to the Lord, "Your people, whom You have brought out" (verse 11). So, as it stood, the people of Israel were in such a state of degradation that neither the Lord Himself nor Moses wanted to be identified with them. We will now continue with the story. God goes on to say to Moses:

> "*They have quickly turned aside from the way which I commanded them. They have made for themselves a molten calf, and have worshiped it and have sacrificed to it and said, 'This is your god, O Israel, who brought you up from the land of Egypt!'" The LORD said to Moses, "I have seen this people, and behold, they are an obstinate people. Now then, let Me alone, that My anger may burn against them and that I may destroy them; and I will make of you a great nation.*"

Moses Responds

Note that phrase, "Let me alone." We will come back to those words in a little while. First let's look at Moses' response:

> *Then Moses entreated the LORD his God, and said, "O LORD, why does Your anger burn against Your people whom You have brought out from the land of Egypt with*

great power and with a mighty hand? [Notice, Moses said, 'Lord, they're not my people, they're Your people whom You have brought out from the land of Egypt.'] *Why should the Egyptians speak, saying, 'With evil intent He brought them out to kill them in the mountains and to destroy them from the face of the earth?' Turn from Your burning anger and change Your mind about doing harm to Your people. Remember Abraham, Isaac, and Israel, Your servants to whom You swore by Yourself, and said to them, 'I will multiply your descendants as the stars of the heavens, and all this land of which I have spoken I will give to your descendants, and they shall inherit it forever.'" So the LORD changed His mind about the harm which He said He would do to His people.*

Let's now pick out the main salient features of this tremendous incident—this outstanding example of the power of intercession. I have already pointed out that neither God nor Moses, at that moment, wanted to be identified with Israel. God said to Moses, "Your people, whom you brought out." Moses said to God, "Your people, whom You have brought out."

We also noted that in verse 10, the Lord said to Moses, "Let Me alone, that My anger may burn against them." Have you considered that? In a way, God was saying, "Moses, if you'll step aside, I'll act. But if you remain there before Me, I can't act."

You see, that is the whole faith of the intercessor—that the intercessor's presence between God and the object of His wrath restrains God's wrath. Let's just imagine Almighty God saying to us, "Let Me alone." How could we stand up to that? But the marvelous fact about Moses was that he would not let God alone. He stayed there. He held on.

What Motivated Moses?

Let's take a moment to look at the motivation of Moses. In their interchange on this situation, God had given Moses the most tremendous promise. He said, "I'll blot these people out and I'll make of you a great nation." How many people would have been delighted with the prospect of becoming the unique head and founder of that great nation? But Moses was not concerned for his own glory; instead he was greatly concerned for God's glory.

When he replied to the Lord, the first point he made was, "If you destroy the people of Israel, then the Egyptians will say You never meant to do Your people good. You brought them out only to do them harm. Think what will happen to Your reputation in the earth." Clearly, Moses was not concerned for his own glory—but he was greatly concerned for God's glory.

Let's also notice the basis of Moses' appeal to God. He appealed to two components: God's Word and God's oath. "Remember," he said, "Your servants to whom You swore by Yourself and said to them, 'I will multiply your descendants.'" What Moses said is really the basis on which the intercessor comes to God: God's Word and God's oath (or His promise). Moses is saying, "God, You're a covenant-keeping God. I trust You to keep that covenant You've made. I believe You won't break it. I'm standing here because I believe that."

God Responds

It is very important for us to notice, as we have already seen in the case of Abraham's intercession, that God responds to the prayers of His servants. In the translation we have quoted here, it says, "The LORD changed His mind." It staggers my own mind—that a man, by his prayer, can cause God to change His mind. Yet the Scriptures indicate that it is so. God wants us to influence Him. He wants to be changed by us in the direction of His highest will. But He waits for us to do it.

By this act of intercession, one man—Moses—saved a whole nation. That is the power and the possibility of intercession.

Moses Intercedes Again

We want to look now at another example of the power of intercession in the life of Moses. In this case, Moses was not the only intercessor. Moses and Aaron became intercessors together. I think this is very significant, because in the previous occasion we studied, Aaron was really the source of the problem. Thankfully, Aaron had progressed in the incident we are about to examine.

Now, he was part of the solution.

The incident we want to study is found in the sixteenth chapter of Numbers. Here is the situation. There had been a growing rebellion among some of the chiefs of the various tribes against the leadership of Moses and Aaron. Some of those leaders had risen up and said, "We are the same kind of people as Moses and Aaron. They have no preeminence over us." At a certain point, God had intervened with a signal judgment against these leaders. He had caused the earth to open and swallow up some of the people who had led this rebellion against Moses and Aaron.

Then, the following day, all the congregation of Israel had turned against Moses and Aaron, accusing them of being responsible for the death of the people who had been swallowed up by the Lord's judgment. We pick up the story in Numbers 16:41:

> *But on the next day all the congregation of the sons of Israel grumbled against Moses and Aaron, saying, "You are the ones who have caused the death of the LORD's peo-*

ple." It came about, however, when the congregation had assembled against Moses and Aaron, that they turned toward the tent of meeting, and behold, the cloud covered it and the glory of the LORD appeared. [God visibly and personally intervened at that point.] Then Moses and Aaron came to the front of the tent of meeting, and the LORD spoke to Moses, saying, "Get away from among this congregation, that I may consume them instantly." Then they fell on their faces. Moses said to Aaron, "Take your censer and put in it fire from the altar, and lay incense on it; then bring it quickly to the congregation and make atonement for them, for wrath has gone forth from the LORD, the plague has begun!" Then Aaron took [the censer] as Moses had spoken, and ran into the midst of the assembly, for behold, the plague had begun among the people. So [Aaron] put on the incense and made atonement for the people. He took his stand between the dead and the living, so that the plague was checked.

A Beautiful Picture

In this concluding section, we will look at some of the outstanding features of the incident just described. First of all, I have to say, I marvel at the patience and longsuffering of Moses. These people had complained and murmured and disobeyed time after time. As a result, God was saying that He was going to destroy them. Instead of agreeing, Moses pleaded with God for them. I think many of us would have perhaps said, "At last, Lord. You've seen what kind of people they are. Go ahead. They deserve it." But not Moses.

The remedy Moses gives to Aaron represents a beautiful picture. Moses tells Aaron to take the censer with the burning coals from off the altar, with the incense on top of the coals going up in a fragrant white smoke. That image typifies the praying heart. The praying heart has to be burning like those coals. As the prayer goes up from a praying heart, it goes up like a fragrant white incense before God.

Let's also notice Aaron's posture. He took his stand between the dead and the living. That is the position of the intercessor—the one who comes in between. We see that where the white incense went up, the plague stopped. That is a picture of what intercessory prayer can do.

Aaron had been part of the problem the first time. Now he was part of the solution. Doesn't that encourage you and me? Doesn't that inspire us to think in terms of moving out in faith and becoming intercessors—wafting up that fragrant white smoke of intercession that can change the situation and save those who are doomed to die?

CHAPTER THREE

Daniel, the Intercessor

In previous chapters, I took examples of the ministry of intercession from the lives of two great servants of God: Abraham and Moses. Certain features emerged that are characteristic of men and women who have mastered this art of intercession. For example, intimacy with God; then, boldness in addressing God; then, conviction of God's absolute justice—both to judge the wicked and to spare the righteous; and finally, a concern for God's glory with, conversely, a corresponding disregard of personal interests and ambition.

The Habit of Prayer

In this chapter, we will turn to another great

servant of God, Daniel. The incident we will focus on is found in the ninth chapter of Daniel. But let's first look at an incident that took place in the sixth chapter, so you can see the background of Daniel's habit of prayer.

Some qualities don't just come automatically—at a moment's notice. There are aspects of our lives that must be carefully cultivated by the right habits—and Daniel was a man who had cultivated the habit of prayer. At this particular point in his career in Daniel 6, he was, as it were, the prime minister of the Persian Empire. However, the men under his authority were jealous of him, so they tried to have him removed from his position. They couldn't find anything to criticize in the way he handled his job, so they knew the only way to eventually get at him was on the basis of his religion.

So, these men persuaded the emperor of Persia to pass a law stipulating that for 30 days, no one was to pray to anyone in that empire except the emperor. Of course, for Daniel as an orthodox conforming Jew, that was an impossible situation. Daniel always prayed to God three times every day with his window open toward Jerusalem. When this new law was passed that made it punishable by death to pray that way, he still went on doing the same. This is what we read in Daniel 6:10:

> *Now when Daniel learned that the decree had been published, he went home to his upstairs room where the windows opened toward Jerusalem. Three times a day he got down on his knees and prayed, giving thanks to his God, just as he had done before.*
>
> (NIV)

Focused Prayer

I want to pick out some features from Daniel's experience as an intercessor which are significant. First of all, "three times a day," every day, speaks of persistence. In addition, that window opened toward Jerusalem speaks of specific focus in prayer. We see then that Daniel is an example of persistent, focused prayer. How important it is that we are persistent! How vital that we focus our prayers on specific objectives which are in line with the will of God!

Second, I want you to see how important prayer was to Daniel. Prayer was so important to him that he would not give it up, even if it meant going to the lions' den.

Third, I want you to see that Daniel's prayers were so effective—and Satan feared Daniel's prayers so much—that the enemy worked to change the laws of the Persian Empire just in order to stop Daniel from praying. It's appropriate for you and me to ask ourselves at this point, "Do our prayers frighten the devil that much that he wants to change the laws?" Maybe they do.

Responding to Revelation

I want to direct our attention now to Daniel chapter 9. The particular incident I want to study in a little more detail appears in the first three verses, where Daniel is speaking:

> *In the first year of Darius son of Xerxes (a Mede by descent), who was made ruler over the Babylonian kingdom—in the first year of his reign, I, Daniel, understood from the Scriptures, according to the word*

of the LORD given to Jeremiah the prophet,
that the desolation of Jerusalem would last
seventy years. So I turned to the Lord God
and pleaded with him in prayer and peti-
tion, in fasting, and in sackcloth and ashes.
(NIV)

One point we need to realize from this passage is that our great source of understanding and direction is the Scriptures. Daniel was not only a man of regular prayer, but clearly he was a man who regularly read the Scriptures. It is so important that at all times, our original and primary source of inspiration, direction and understanding of the will of God should come from the Scriptures.

A second point I want you to see is how Daniel responded to the revelation he found in the Scripture. From his reading, he concluded that the desolation of the city of Jerusalem was to last seventy years. In his position of influence and authority in the Persian Empire, he had access to records of the empire and knew that the seventy years had almost run their course. To

Daniel, that sent the message that it was time for God to restore the Jewish people to Jerusalem and to build up the city of Jerusalem again.

When some people get a revelation from the Scripture, it goes to their heads. They become opinionated or they become super-spiritual. They tell everybody how much they have discovered in the Scripture. They take it upon themselves to explain God's plans and God's purposes.

Personally, I don't believe revelation is given to make us feel super-spiritual. In that regard, I find that Daniel responded to this revelation by appropriate action. He didn't simply say, "Isn't that interesting? God is soon going to restore Jerusalem." He saw that this revelation placed a personal responsibility upon him. If it was God's purpose to restore Jerusalem, then it was Daniel's duty to move in and associate himself with the purpose of God. He had a responsibility to commit himself in prayer and in fasting to what God intended to do.

Meeting the Conditions

The passage we read in Daniel 9 says that Daniel discovered from the Scriptures that the desolation of Jerusalem was to last seventy years. It is important to ask ourselves: "Where did Daniel find this in the Scriptures?"

One Scripture where this is clearly stated is Jeremiah 29:10–13. This prophecy of Jeremiah was undoubtedly available to Daniel at that time. Let's read these verses:

> *This is what the LORD says: "When seventy years are completed for Babylon, I will come to you* [the Jewish people] *and fulfill my gracious promise to bring you back to this place* [Jerusalem]. *For I know the plans I have for you," declares the LORD, "plans to prosper you and not to harm you, plans to give you hope and a future. Then you will call upon me and come and pray to me, and I will listen to you. You will seek me and find me when you seek me with all your heart."*
>
> *(NIV)*

This prophecy of Jeremiah holds a clear indication that after seventy years God would begin to restore the Jewish people to Jerusalem and to restore the city itself. Through Jeremiah, God was saying, "I'm ready to do it at the end of seventy years. But you, My people, are going to have to meet My conditions. You're going to have to call upon Me and pray. When you do pray, I'll listen to you."

Daniel knew that his task was not merely to discover an interesting revelation—that the time had come to restore Jerusalem. He also realized that his responsibility was to fulfill the part it outlined—for God's people to pray. Daniel recognized God's emphasis upon prayer. In effect, the Lord was saying, "You're going to have to pray in a special way. You're really going to have to pray."

As the Lord said in these verses, "You will seek Me and find Me when you seek Me with all your heart." In other words, He was saying, "When you give yourself unreservedly to seeking Me and to prayer, then I will respond and do what I've committed Myself to do."

Mourn, Pray, Fast

Daniel doubtless read those words: "When you seek Me with all your heart." How did he respond? We read it in Daniel's own words: "I turned to the Lord God and pleaded with him in prayer and petition, in fasting, and in sackcloth and ashes" (Daniel 9:3 NIV).

In Daniel's day, sackcloth and ashes were the recognized marks of mourning. So Daniel, in a sense, became a mourner. He mourned the desolation of Jerusalem.

There is a kind of godly mourning which is very close to the heart of God. Jesus said in the Sermon on the Mount, "Blessed are those who mourn, for they will be comforted" (Matthew 5:4 NIV). Isaiah 61:3 has this promise of God for those who mourn in Zion: He will give them "beauty for ashes, the oil of joy for mourning, the garment of praise for the spirit of heaviness." What is described in these verses is not self-centered grief. It is the act of mourning over God's people and the situation of God's city. It is mourning "in Zion." Daniel was that kind of a mourner—and it meant much to God.

Not only did Daniel mourn and pray, but he also fasted. God says in 2 Chronicles 7:14:

". . . if my people, who are called by my name, will humble themselves and pray and seek my face and turn from their wicked ways, then will I hear from heaven and will forgive their sin and will heal their land."

(*NIV*)

Scripturally it is clear that there is a certain, specific way God has ordained for His people to humble themselves before Him. What is that way? By fasting.

How Do We Pray?

In the final section of this chapter, I want to show you the kind of prayer Daniel offered out of this situation of mourning, fasting, and seeking God with all his heart. It is a very important pattern for us. We see it in Daniel 9:4 and following, where Daniel says:

I prayed to the LORD my God and con-
fessed: "O Lord, the great and awesome
God, who keeps his covenant of love with
all who love him and obey his commands,
we have sinned and done wrong. We have
been wicked and have rebelled; we have
turned away from your commands and
laws. We have not listened to your serv-
ants the prophets, who spoke in your
name to our kings, our princes and our
fathers, and to all the people of the land.
Lord, you are righteous, but this day we
are covered with shame."

(NIV)

I want you to notice how the word "we"
occurs again and again in that short passage of
prayer. Daniel was one of the most righteous
men of all those whose lives have been recorded
in Scripture. In fact, there is no actual sin recorded in the Bible's account of the life of Daniel.

In his prayers to the Lord, Daniel could have
easily taken a self-righteous attitude concerning
his fellow Israelites. He could have said, "These

are wicked people. These are people who deserve Your judgment." But he didn't. Instead, he identified himself with God's people. He took his place with them and said, "We have sinned. We have failed. Judgment belongs to us."

Take a moment and contrast this response with the Pharisee who went up into the temple to pray. Do you remember what he prayed? "God, I thank You that I am not like all other men" (Luke 18:11 NIV). Let me ask you: Which kind of prayer reaches the heart of God? Here is what I believe: Not the prayer of the Pharisee, but the prayer of the man who was fasting and mourning. God responds to the prayer of the one who casts himself without reservation on the mercy of God, identifying himself with the needs of God's people.

What a vital lesson for us as we respond in prayer to what God shows us in His Word!

Chapter Four

Esther, the Intercessor

In our previous chapters, we have examined three examples of the ministry of intercession. These examples were set by three great servants of God: Abraham, Moses and Daniel. Certain features have emerged from our exploration of these examples which characterize men and women who have mastered this art of intercession.

Let's take a moment to recap some of those features.

First, a relationship of intimacy with God.

Second, a boldness in approaching God.

Third, a conviction of God's absolute justice, both positive and negative—that God will spare the righteous but judge the wicked.

Fourth, a concern for God's glory and, conversely, a disregard of personal interests and ambitions.

Fifth, a dedication to the task of intercession even at the cost of life itself—even if it means the lions' den.

Sixth, a willingness to identify with those for whom we intercede. As we pointed out, this kind of praying is not like that of the Pharisee who said, "God, I thank You that I am not like other men" (Luke 18:11 NIV). Rather, this kind of praying identifies itself with those for whom we pray. We say, "*We* have sinned," not "*They* have sinned."

Background on Esther

For our fourth example of the ministry of intercession, we will look in this chapter at the story of Queen Esther. The incident we are going to study is taken from chapter four of the book of Esther. Before we begin our study, we need to fill in briefly the historical background.

Esther was a beautiful Jewish maiden in the time of the exile of the Jewish people to the Persian Empire from their land and from the city of Jerusalem. She was an orphan who had been brought up by her uncle, Mordecai, who was actually an important official in the court of the Persian emperor. At a certain point, Esther had been chosen to become the new queen of the Persian Empire. Clearly, she had been raised up to a position of tremendous influence and importance in the Emperor's or King's palace. However, Esther had never publicly revealed the fact that she was Jewish.

After Esther had been raised up as queen, a certain anti-Semite, an official in the court of the Persian Emperor named Haman, hatched a plot. Haman had obtained authorization from the emperor that on a certain day at a future time, there would be a "pogrom," or organized massacre, of the Jewish people. By this edict, Jews in the entire Persian Empire would all be destroyed. Haman's plan was nothing less than total genocide—annihilation of the entire Jewish nation. At that time, it is probable that all the Jews in the world were living within the borders of the Persian Empire. So what the Jews faced was an extremely desperate situation.

When this decree instigated by Haman went forth, Mordecai sent an urgent message to Esther in the queen's palace. He informed Esther that it was her responsibility to get to the king and persuade him to change his mind about the decree. Esther sent word back that she had not had any access to the king for quite a while. But the response came again from Mordecai to Esther that she was duty-bound to go to the king on behalf of her people.

The exchange between Esther and Mordecai and what resulted from it is what we will now examine in Esther 4:11–17:

> *"All the king's officials and the people of the royal provinces know that for any man or woman who approaches the king in the inner court without being summoned the king has but one law: that he be put to death. The only exception to this is for the king to extend the gold scepter to him and spare his life. But thirty days have passed since I was called to go to the king." When Esther's words were reported to Mordecai,*

he sent back this answer: "Do not think that because you are in the king's house you alone of all the Jews will escape. For if you remain silent at this time, relief and deliverance for the Jews will arise from another place, but you and your father's family will perish. And who knows but that you have come to royal position for such a time as this?" Then Esther sent this reply to Mordecai: "Go, gather together all the Jews who are in Susa [the capital city], *and fast for me. Do not eat or drink for three days, night or day. I and my maids will fast as you do. When this is done, I will go to the king, even though it is against the law. And if I perish, I perish." So Mordecai went away and carried out all of Esther's instructions.*

(NIV)

Here again is the biblical picture of an intercessor. Note the commitment: "If I perish, I perish." In other words, "Whether I live or die is not the most important question. The most important issue is that I do what I can on behalf of my people."

Our Willingness to Respond

Please note what Mordecai said to Esther: "Who knows but that you have come to royal position for such a time as this?" This perspective applies as well to us, as Christians. We are a kingdom of priests. We have come to royal position. We cannot turn away from our responsibilities and be indifferent any more than Esther could.

We must be willing to identify ourselves with the rest of God's people. We cannot hide away in some palace and say, "Well, this crisis doesn't concern me." We must be like Daniel and like Esther—willing to lay down our lives, to risk all, to stand by the people of God, to identify ourselves with God's purposes, to take up the prayer burden.

This passage we have just studied implies that Esther, just like Daniel, knew that there are times when praying alone is not enough. Esther said, "Not only must we pray, but all of us will have to fast three days and three nights. And after we've prayed and fasted, then I'll go in to the king and see what comes to pass."

In the passage that follows (Esther 5:1–3), we will read about Esther's action to approach the king.

On the third day Esther put on her royal robes and stood in the inner court of the palace, [I like that phrase, "the inner court." Intercession always means coming into the inner court, into the immediate presence of the Lord. So Esther stood in the inner court of the palace] *in front of the king's hall. The king was sitting on his royal throne in the hall, facing the entrance. When he saw Queen Esther standing in the court, he was pleased with her and held out to her the gold scepter that was in his hand.* [That was the evidence that he was prepared to show mercy—that he would not apply the law that she was to be put to death.] *So Esther approached and touched the tip of the scepter.* [By that act, she availed herself of the mercy the king was offering. I think that's something we must also learn to do—to go into God's presence and when He stretches out the scepter of mercy, we have to touch the tip of the scepter.] *Then the king asked, "What is it, Queen Esther? What is your request? Even up to half the kingdom, it will be given you."*

(NIV)

Esther Prevails

This passage above is the record that Esther had prevailed. The rest of the book of Esther is the unfolding of the outcome of her intercession. However, the point at which the victory was won for the Jewish people was when Esther, at the risk of her own life, had gained the attention of the king by her intercession. The victory, I believe, is always won in intercession. That is the place where history is made. That is where the course and destiny of nations are changed. That is where we become the kind of rulers God wants us to be.

I want you to recognize this beautiful additional fact about Esther: when she went in to the king, she didn't go in as a beggar. She didn't grovel. She put on her royal robes and stood there in his presence as a beautiful and lovely queen.

This is important for us to see—that Esther went in like a queen. She put on her royal apparel. She recognized who she was. She took her rightful position. I believe the same applies to you and me as Christians. We have to recognize who we are in God's sight—understanding the position to which God has elevated us. We are not to grovel. We are not to go as beggars.

Ruling in Prayer

We need to pay attention to the following beautiful words from Isaiah 52:

> *Awake, awake, O Zion, clothe yourself with strength. Put on your garments of splendor, O Jerusalem, the holy city. The uncircumcised and defiled will not enter you again. Shake off your dust; rise up, sit enthroned, O Jerusalem. Free yourself from the chains on your neck, O captive Daughter of Zion.*
>
> (*NIV*)

I believe those verses are a challenge to us about the way we pray. We are to become what God says we are. We are to get out of the dust. We are to arise and sit on the throne God has offered us that we may rule with Him in prayer and intercession.

Please notice some of the truths this passage implies. First of all, what we must put on. We must put on strength and beauty. A magnificent verse—Psalm 96:6—encourages us in this regard:

> *Splendor and majesty are before him; strength and glory are in his sanctuary.*
>
> (NIV)

God wants us to put on the strength and the glory that are appropriate to His sanctuary and to His inner court. As the passage from Isaiah 52 implies, we must put away all that defiles. Symbolically it says "the uncircumcised and the defiled will not enter." We have to be pure.

Similarly, we must put away all that binds. We are to loose ourselves from the chains on our neck. What kinds of chains bind us when we come to God in prayer? I believe they are chains such as doubt, unbelief, fear, as well as wrong attitudes and relationships. We are to release ourselves from these chains.

Having released ourselves, we are then to take decisive action. We are to arise. We must not lie there and grovel any longer. We must realize the kind of persons we are in God. According to our destiny in Him, we are to rise up and be the people God desires us to be.

A Significant Nuance

As we close this chapter, it is important for us to return to the story of Esther for a moment. Esther had taken the place of a previous queen, Vashti, who had been deposed. Why had Vashti been deposed as queen? The king had held a great banquet in celebration, and at the climax to the banquet, he wanted to present the queen in all her beauty to his people. However, Vashti was attending her own banquet and she refused to come. For that reason, she was deposed as queen.

Very simply, I want to point out to you the difference between Vashti and Esther as queens.

I'll express it this way: Vashti put her own plans and activities before the wishes of the king; but Esther put the wishes of the king and the need of her people before her own life and desires.

I believe those truths contrasting Vashti and Esther apply to the church today. So many times, the church is more like Vashti—busy with its own programs, its own plans, its own preoccupations, not open to what the king has to say. I pray that we may become a church like Queen Esther—putting the will of the king and the needs of our fellow people before our own lives, if necessary.

Here is the point we must remember: Esther's intercession shaped the course of history. You and I must realize that we can do the same.

In our concluding chapter, I will continue with this theme of intercession, showing you how to apply it in a practical way to your own life.

CHAPTER FIVE

Will You Be an Intercessor?

In this concluding chapter, I want to begin by reminding you of the definition of intercession which I gave earlier in this book. The intercessor is the one who comes in between. That is the literal meaning of the word. The intercessor comes in between God and the objects of God's just wrath and impending judgment. In doing so, that person says, in effect, "God, You have every right to strike these people. Your justice demands that You do so. But I'm standing between You and them. Lord, in all reverence, but with great boldness, I want to say that if You strike them, You are going to have to strike me first." That is the position of the intercessor.

Features of Intercession

In our earlier chapters, we have taken examples of this ministry of intercession from four great servants of God: Abraham, Moses, Daniel and Esther. Certain features have emerged from these examples which characterize men and women who have mastered the art of intercession. Let me list some of these features briefly for you, with a few references to those who best represent each feature.

The first feature is an intimacy with God. I believe we see this trait particularly in Abraham and in Moses. They talked to God just like a man talks to his friend.

The second feature is boldness. Both Abraham and Moses spoke out to God. They really, in a sense, almost challenged Almighty God.

The third feature is conviction of God's absolute justice. This we see particularly in Abraham and in Daniel, who freely acknowledged that God's judgment on His people was entirely just.

The fourth feature is a concern for God's glory—and conversely, a disregard of personal interests and ambitions. We see this particularly in Moses. In His wrath with the people of Israel, God had said to Moses, "I'll make of you a great nation." But Moses was much more concerned for God's reputation than for his own.

The fifth feature is dedication to the task, even at the cost of life itself. Both Daniel and Esther literally had to risk their own lives to fulfill their ministry of intercession.

The sixth feature is a willingness to identify with those for whom we intercede. Again, we see this particularly in Daniel and in Esther. You will remember that I contrasted this attitude with the prayer of the Pharisee that Jesus cites in the New Testament—the man who said, "God, I thank You that I am not like other men." That self-righteous attitude is totally inconsistent with the spirit of the intercessor.

For Lack of an Intercessor

So far in this book, we have studied situations where God found an intercessor—and consequently the situation was saved, or a nation was saved, and history was changed. What does the

Bible have to say about situations where there was no intercessor?

We are going to examine that issue in this chapter. In doing so, the first passage we will look at is Isaiah 59. This chapter represents a terrible catalog of the sins and the backslidings of God's people, Israel. It is a picture of almost unredeemed and unrelieved failure and wickedness.

The account is presented in the first person plural. In other words, it is an acknowledgement by the people of their own condition. We will begin at Isaiah 59:12:

> *For our offenses are many in your sight, and our sins testify against us. Our offenses are ever with us, and we acknowledge our iniquities: rebellion and treachery against the LORD, turning our backs on our God, fomenting oppression and revolt, uttering lies our hearts have conceived. So justice is driven back, and righteousness stands at a distance; truth has stumbled in the streets, honesty cannot enter. Truth is nowhere to be found, and whoever shuns evil becomes*

a prey. [What a terrible situation. Now we see God's reaction in the middle of verse 15:] *The Lord looked and was displeased that there was no justice. He saw that there was no one, and he was appalled that there was no one to intercede ...*

(*NIV*)

Isn't that an amazing statement? Let's repeat that phrase to get its full impact: "God was appalled that there was no one to intercede."

To me, it seems that the worst part of the entire situation was not the wickedness of the people, although that was bad enough. The final realization that caused God to be appalled—that He could hardly conceive—was that there was no one to intercede. To me, that would seem to be the final evidence of backsliding and hardness of heart in the people of God—when there is no one left to intercede. In my estimation that would be the point at which the situation must truly be called hopeless.

As long as there is an intercessor, there is hope. But where there is no more intercessor, we would have to conclude on the basis of Scripture that there is no more hope. The one person God looks for in such a crisis is the intercessor.

The Need for Cleansing

We have just looked at the situation in Isaiah chapter 59 where the nation was totally corrupt and there was no intercessor. This was the condition which caused God to be appalled. Let's now look at a similar situation portrayed in Ezekiel chapter 22. This is somewhat later in the history of Israel, but a similar type of situation. Beginning at Ezekiel 22:23, the prophet says:

> *And the word of the LORD came to me saying, "Son of man, say to her* [the land of Israel], *'You are a land that is not cleansed or rained on in the day of indignation.'"*

Once when I was pondering this Scripture, it came to me very vividly that when a land is wicked and backslidden, the only element that can cleanse it is the rain. Not the literal rain, but the rain of God's Holy Spirit.

I have often taught on the encouragement from the book of Hosea: "It is time to seek the LORD until He comes to rain righteousness upon you" (Hosea 10:12). That is the kind of rain that can cleanse a land. I personally believe it is the only kind of rain that can cleanse our land—or any other nation in a similar condition.

Order of Responsibility

As Ezekiel 22 progresses, it contains a catalog of the failure of every section of God's people in this situation. We find that there are four categories of people listed. By coincidence, in the English language, each of them begins with the letter *p*. They are prophets, priests, princes and people.

It is significant that God begins His catalog of wrongdoing with the prophets and with the priests. The princes I take to be the secular rulers. But God doesn't lay the blame primarily at the door of the secular rulers. He lays the blame primarily at the door of the spiritual leaders: the prophets and the priests.

By way of definition, the prophet is the one

whose responsibility it is to declare the counsel of God to God's people. The priest is the one who cares for the daily life of the congregation of God's people.

In the verses that follow, let's see what God says about prophets, priests, princes and then all the people. Ezekiel 22:25–31:

> *"There is a conspiracy of her prophets in her midst, like a roaring lion tearing the prey. . . . Her priests have done violence to My law and have profaned My holy things. . . . Her princes within her are like wolves tearing the prey. . . . Her prophets have smeared whitewash for them, seeing false visions and divining lies for them. . . .* [Notice the prophets, instead of reproving the wickedness, have covered it up with false excuses and religious talk.] *The people of the land have practiced oppression and committed robbery. . . ."*

All sections of the entire nation are held guilty before God: the prophets, the priests, the princes and the people. What was the general characteristic of their failure? What was the general guilt of all of them? I would sum it up in one phrase: "the ruthless pursuit of selfish ends." Everyone was putting his own gain and his own selfish ends before those of his fellow men—and certainly before the interests of God.

Looking for Intercessors

How did God respond to this desperate situation of wickedness? We read the answer to that question in the two closing verses of the chapter: verses 30 and 31. God is speaking, and He says:

> *"I searched for a man among them who would build up the wall and stand in the gap before Me for the land, that I would not destroy it; but I found no one. Thus [or, therefore] I have poured out My indignation on them; I have consumed them with the fire of My wrath; their way I have brought upon their heads," declares the Lord God.*

In this desperate situation, God did not look for a large group. He did not necessarily go to the rulers or even the prophets or the priests. He looked for one person. What kind of a person? Someone who would stand in the gap before Him for the land.

What kind of a person is it who stands in the gap before God for a land, for a city, for a nation? It is an intercessor. I suppose that one of the most tragic statements of Scripture appears there at the end of verse 30 where God says, "I found no one." To me, that verse seems to indicate that even in that desperate situation, one intercessor could have changed the whole course of history. One intercessor could have prevailed with God to the sparing of the judgment that came upon God's people.

But when God could find no intercessor, then there was no more hope. Let me say that again. As long as there is an intercessor there is hope. But when there is no intercessor, there is no more hope.

How do you see your land today? How do you see your nation? In many ways, isn't your nation at present very much like the situation in Ezekiel's day? Isn't there guilt and failure on the part of almost every section of the populace—the prophets, the priests, the secular rulers, and the people at large?

What is the situation? What is God's response? I believe God is looking for a man or woman to stand in the gap. I believe He is looking for someone to make up the hedge—a man or a woman. An intercessor. Will you offer yourself to God for this ministry?

It's Your Time

Maybe as you have read the teaching in this book, you have sensed a stirring inside of you. Maybe you have felt a nudge from the Holy Spirit that God is calling you into the action of prayer and intercession. Or maybe you have sensed a renewal of God's call upon your life in this area. Maybe you had pulled back in discouragement, but now feel Him drawing you to re-engage.

My encouragement to you at this moment would be that instead of resisting this urge, that you yield yourself to the Lord and to His destiny for your life. You can do so by praying the following prayer:

> *Dear Lord, I have read this teaching and I have seen the examples in Your Word of those who have yielded their lives to You in intercession. Lord, I want to be counted among their number.*
>
> *I come to You now, in the name of Jesus, and I offer myself to You. I make myself available to pray for situations You want me to pray for, and I will intercede for them at Your direction. I am fully Yours, Lord. I give myself to You. Amen.*

Thank you for responding to the Lord in this way. May you experience His blessing and favor as you intercede in obedience to Him.

ABOUT THE AUTHOR

Derek Prince (1915–2003) was born in India of British parents. Educated as a scholar of Greek and Latin at Eton College and Cambridge University, England, he held a Fellowship in Ancient and Modern Philosophy at King's College. He also studied several modern languages, including Hebrew and Aramaic, at Cambridge University and the Hebrew University in Jerusalem.

While serving with the British army in World War II, he began to study the Bible and experienced a life-changing encounter with Jesus Christ. Out of this encounter he formed two conclusions: first, that Jesus Christ is alive; second, that the Bible is a true, relevant, up-to-date book. These conclusions altered the whole course of his life, which he then devoted to studying and teaching the Bible.

Derek's main gift of explaining the Bible and its teaching in a clear and simple way has helped build a foundation of faith in millions of lives. His non-denominational, non-sectarian approach has made his teaching equally relevant and helpful to people from all racial and religious backgrounds.

He is the author of over 50 books, 600 audio and 110 video teachings, many of which have been translated and published in more than 100 languages. His daily radio broadcast is translated into Arabic, Bahasa (Indonesia), Chinese, Croatian, German, Malagasy, Mongolian, Russian, Spanish and Tongan, The radio program continues to touch lives around the world.

Derek Prince Ministries persists in reaching out to believers in over 140 countries with Derek's teachings, fulfilling the mandate to keep on "until Jesus returns." This is effected through the outreaches of more than 45 Derek Prince offices around the world, including primary work in Australia, Canada, China, France, Germany, the Netherlands, New Zealand, Norway, Russia,

South Africa, Switzerland, the United Kingdom and the United States. For current information about these and other worldwide locations, visit www.derekprince.com.

Inspired by Derek's teaching?
Help make it available to others!

If you have been inspired and blessed by this Derek Prince resource you can help make it available to a spiritually hungry believer in other countries, such as China, the Middle East, India, Africa or Russia.

Even a small gift from you will ensure that that a pastor, a Bible college student or a believer elsewhere in the world receives a free copy of a Derek Prince resource in their own language.

Donate now: www.dpmuk.org/give

More best-sellers by Derek Prince

- Blessing Or Curse: You Can Choose
- Bought With Blood
- Christ's Last Order
- Foundational Truths For Christian Living
- Life-Changing Spiritual Power
- Marriage Covenant
- Prayers & Proclamations
- Self-Study Bible Course
- Spiritual Warfare For The End Times
- They Shall Expel Demons
- Who Is The Holy Spirit?

SHAPING HISTORY THROUGH PRAYER AND FASTING

Christians have altered the course of history and governments by emphasizing biblical methods of prayer and fasting.
Best-selling author and Bible teacher Derek Prince recounts from personal experience how history was shaped through prayer during the Second World War in North Africa, at the birth of the State of Israel, at the end of the Stalin era, and at the time that Kenya attained independence. Learn how you can implement change – in your family, church, locale, country, and the world.

Paperback and ebook
978-1-782633-10-5
£ 8.99

www.dpmuk.org/shop

Spiritual Warfare for the End Times

As the time approaches for Jesus' return, the spiritual battle between good and evil is heating up. The enemy is on the move. Yet God is on the move, too, in powerful ways – and you can join Him in His work.
With piercing insight and practical application, Derek Prince will help you understand not only the intensified warfare environment in which we live, but also how you can help unleash God's goodness in the world.

Paperback and ebook
978-1-78263-470-6
£ 9.99

www.dpmuk.org/shop

DEREK PRINCE MINISTRIES OFFICES WORLDWIDE

DPM – Asia/Pacific
admin@dpm.co.nz
www.dpm.co.nz

DPM – Australia
enquiries@au.derekprince.com
www.derekprince.com.au

DPM – Canada
enquiries.dpm@eastlink.ca
www.derekprince.org

DPM – France
info@derekprince.fr
www.derekprince.fr

DPM – Germany
ibl@ibl-dpm.net
www.ibl-dpm.net

DPM Indian Subcontinent
secretary@derekprince.in
www.derekprince.in

DPM – Middle East
contact@dpm.name
www.dpm.name

DPM – Netherlands
info@derekprince.nl
www.derekprince.nl

DPM – Norway
xpress@dpskandinavia.com
www.derekprince.no

Derek Prince Publications Pte. Ltd.
dpmchina@singnet.com.sg
www.dpmchina.org (English)
www.ygmweb.org (Chinese)

DPM – Russia/Caucasus
dpmrussia@gmail.com
www.derekprince.ru

DPM – South Africa
enquiries@derekprince.co.za
www.derekprince.co.za

DPM – Switzerland
dpm-ch@ibl-dpm.net
www.ibl-dpm.net

DPM – UK
enquiries@dpmuk.org
www.dpmuk.org

DPM – USA
ContactUs@derekprince.org
www.derekprince.org

Milton Keynes UK
Ingram Content Group UK Ltd.
UKHW041319170324
439648UK00007B/294

9 781782 637479